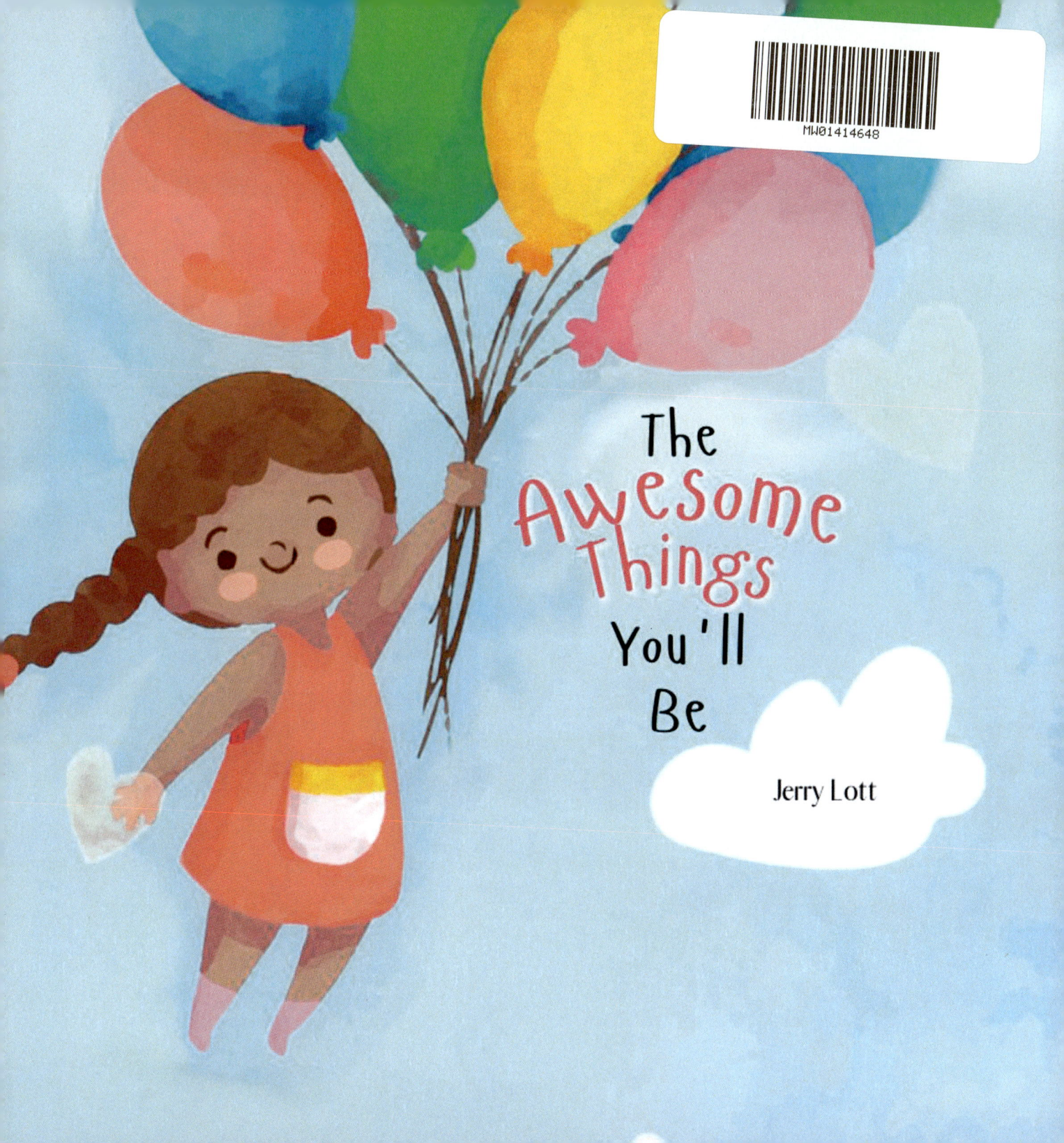

Copyright © 2022 by Jerry Lott

All rights reserved. No part of this book may be reproduced or used in any manner without written permission of the copyright owner except for the use of quotations in a book review. For more information, address: Sinjressforall@gmail.com Designs and pictures were taken from freepik.com/Designed by brgfx under freemium license, vecteezy.com under freemium license, Creativefabrica.com under premium license, and Canva.com under premium.

This book is dedicated to all awesome girls

Oh sweet and smart child of mine
Of the sweetest heart and the brightest mind

I wonder and wonder what the future will hold
For someone so smart and bright, and brave and bold

I'm sure you'll shine left and right
Then shine forever day and night

You will be unique and special, this much is true
And again I wonder what awesome things you will do

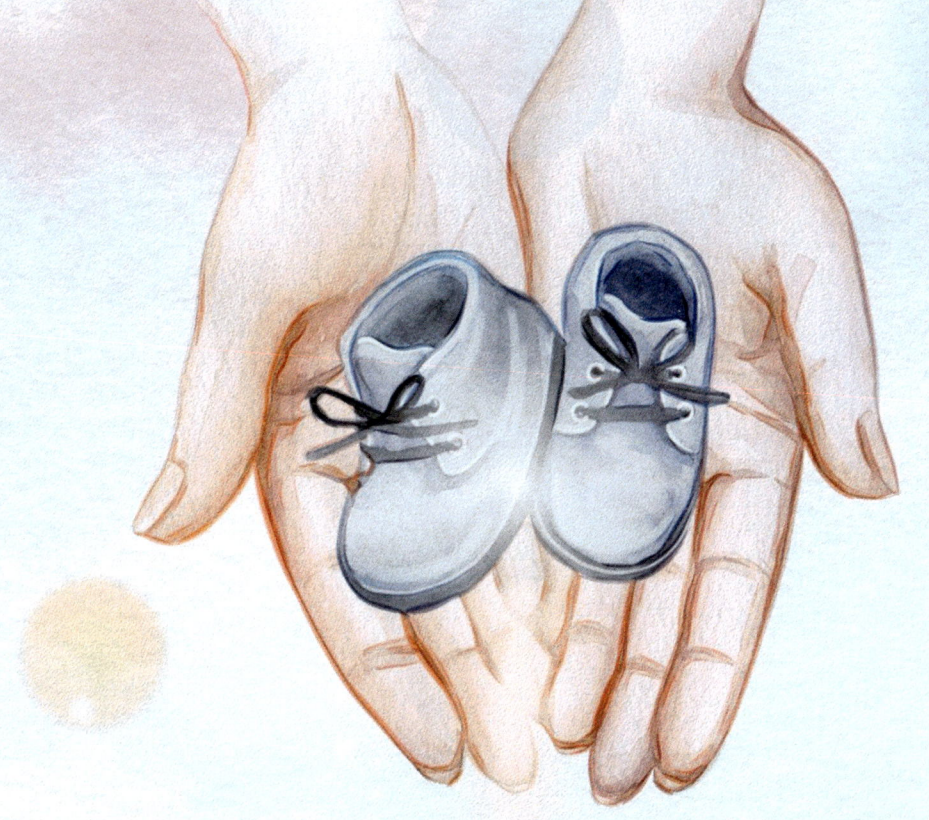

Will you, in glory and grace,

Roam the whole wide space?

Or will you fly and fly

Very sky high?

That no one could beat

Or your designs will be the best

And so, everyone will be impressed

Or you might for everyone's sake

big discoveries make

Oh my dear child of the sweetest heart and the brightest mind

Will you fight and fight

For every right?

Or will you create the best software

With skill and flair?

Or will your clothing line

be a luxury sign?

Maybe you'll report the news

And do the best interviews

Or so well and quick

Will you cure the sick?

Will you solemnly swear

To rule fair and square?

And day and night

Every crime you'll fight

Or will you write and move people to tears

And bring them joy and cheers?

Oh sweet and smart child of mine

Will you be the best vet

To treat every pet?

Will be the best of the best

Or people will follow you along

And they'll be fit and strong

Will your songs be heard and heard

And hearts will be stirred?

Or will the roles you play

memories

In memory stay?

And many more and more things you can certainly be
Flying so high, roaming the land, or sailing the sea

Oh sweet and smart child of mine
Of the sweetest heart and the brightest mind

You'll shine so bright whatever you'll do
And whatever you'll become, I will always love you

Made in the USA
Las Vegas, NV
25 July 2024